S0-FEO-054

TURKEY DRUMS AND SAUERKRAUT

2 tbs (30 ml) vegetable oil
1 medium onion, sliced thin
1 medium green apple, cored, sliced thin
2 small carrots, halved
1 garlic clove, minced
2 lbs (910 g) sauerkraut, rinsed, squeezed dry, divided
2 turkey drumsticks
1 lb (455 g) EMPIRE KOSHER Turkey Kielbasa, cut into 2-inch pieces
¾ cup (180 ml) dry kosher white wine
¾ cup (180 ml) kosher chicken broth
2 tbs (30 ml) gin
½ tsp (3 ml) salt
¼ tsp (1 ml) pepper

In a large 4-qt pot heat the oil; add onion, apple, carrots, and garlic. Cook until onion is soft, about 3 minutes. Add half the sauerkraut, place drums and kielbasa on top of sauerkraut. Top with remaining sauerkraut. Pour in wine, chicken broth, gin, season with salt and pepper. Cover, simmer until drumsticks are tender, about 1½ hours. Serves 4.

Approximate nutritional analysis per serving: Calories 711, Protein 71 g, Carbohydrates 24 g, Fat 32 g, Cholesterol 205 mg, Sodium 210 mg

CRANBERRY CHICKEN

1 - 3–4 lb (1.4–1.8 kg) EMPIRE KOSHER Chicken
1 cup (240 ml) flour
salt and pepper to taste
dash cayenne pepper
1 cup (240 ml) oil for frying
1 - 16 oz can (480 g) whole cranberry sauce
¼ cup (60 ml) chopped onion
¾ cup (180 ml) orange juice
¼ tsp (1 ml) ground cinnamon
¼ tsp (1 ml) ginger

Cut chicken into serving pieces, rinse in cold water, and pat dry. Mix flour with salt and peppers and dust each piece. Pan-fry in oil until brown, turning once. Remove chicken, drain all but 1 tbs of fat. Mix remaining ingredients in a small saucepan and bring to a boil. Return chicken to pan, pour sauce over chicken, cover and simmer for 45 minutes or until chicken is very tender. Serves 4.

Approximate nutritional analysis per serving: Calories 773, Protein 100 g, Carbohydrates 15 g, Fat 32 g, Cholesterol 301 mg, Sodium 295 mg

ARROZ CON POLLO
Chicken with Yellow Rice

2 tbs (30 ml) GOYA Olive Oil
4–6 cut-up chicken pieces
2 cups (480 ml) water
1 pkg. GOYA Yellow Rice
½ cup (120 ml) frozen peas
1 whole GOYA Pimiento, sliced

Heat olive oil in a skillet and sauté chicken pieces until browned. Drain excess oil, add water to skillet, and bring to a boil. Add rice and contents of seasoning packet. Cover and simmer 25 minutes. A few minutes before done, add peas. Garnish with pimiento slices. Serves 4.

Approximate nutritional analysis per serving: Calories 793, Protein 87 g, Carbohydrates 43 g, Fat 28 g, Cholesterol 251 mg, Sodium 513 mg

Opposite: Arroz con Pollo

HUNTER-STYLE CHICKEN

4 slices bacon, cut into 1-inch pieces
1 medium onion, sliced
1 tbs (15 ml) vegetable oil
2–2½ lbs (910–1138 g) broiler-fryer pieces
1 - 16 oz can (480 g) tomatoes, cut into bite-size pieces
⅓ cup (80 ml) HEINZ 57 Sauce
⅛ tsp (.5 ml) pepper
hot cooked rice or noodles

In large skillet, sauté bacon until crisp. Remove bacon; drain fat. Sauté onion in oil until tender; remove. In same skillet, brown chicken, adding more oil if necessary. Drain excess fat. Combine bacon, onion, tomatoes, 57 Sauce, and pepper; pour over chicken. Cover; simmer 20–25 minutes or until chicken is tender, basting occasionally. Remove chicken. Skim excess fat from sauce. If thicker sauce is desired, gradually stir in mixture of equal parts flour and water, simmering until thickened. Serve chicken and sauce with rice or noodles. Serves 4.

Approximate nutritional analysis per serving w/o skin: Calories 410, Protein 44 g, Carbohydrates 20 g, Fat 17 g, Cholesterol 129 mg, Sodium 754 mg

VEAL STEW WITH MUSHROOMS

½ cup (120 ml) chopped onion
¼ cup (60 ml) chopped celery
¼ cup (60 ml) diced carrot
1 garlic clove, finely chopped
2 tsp (10 ml) BERTOLLI Classico Olive Oil
1 lb (455 g) well-trimmed veal shoulder or leg, cut into 1-inch cubes
3 large white button or shitake mushroom caps, quartered
salt and freshly ground black pepper
1 - 14½ oz can (435 g) Italian plum tomatoes with juices
1 cup (240 ml) chicken broth
1 strip orange zest, 2x½ inch
½ tsp (3 ml) dried rosemary
8 oz (240 g) potatoes, peeled and cut into 1-inch cubes
2 cups (480 ml) thick sliced zucchini

In large non-stick skillet, combine the onion, celery, carrot, garlic, and olive oil. Cook, stirring, over low heat until vegetables are tender, about 10 minutes. Add veal and mushrooms with salt and pepper; cook, turning, 5 minutes. Add the tomatoes, broth, orange zest, and rosemary. Cover and cook over medium-low heat, stirring occasionally, until the veal is tender, about 45 minutes. Add the potatoes; cover and cook until potatoes are almost tender, about 10 minutes. Add zucchini, cook 5 minutes. Season to taste. Serves 4.

Approximate nutritional analysis per serving: Calories 234, Protein 26 g, Carbohydrates 18 g, Fat 7 g, Cholesterol 98 mg, Sodium 447 mg

Opposite:
Veal Stew with Mushrooms

BRAISED VEAL BRISKET WITH DRIED FRUIT

1 tbs (15 ml) vegetable oil, divided
2–2½ lb (910–1138 g) veal brisket
2 medium onions, thinly sliced
1 large clove garlic, crushed
1 tsp (5 ml) salt
½ tsp (3 ml) coarse grind black pepper
apple juice
water
3 large carrots, cut into 3x¼x¼-inch strips
2 medium parsnips, cut into 3x¼x¼-inch strips
¾ cup (180 ml) dried pitted prunes
½ cup (120 ml) dried apricot halves
2 tsp (10 ml) cornstarch

Heat 2 tsp oil in Dutch oven over medium-high heat; brown veal brisket on both sides. Remove brisket; reserve. Add remaining 1 tsp oil to Dutch oven, if necessary. Add onions and garlic; cook over medium-low heat 5 minutes or until onions are tender, stirring occasionally. Place brisket, fat side up, on top of onions. Sprinkle with salt and pepper. Pour 6 tbs each apple juice and water around veal. Cover tightly and cook in 450°F (230°C) oven 30 minutes. Reduce heat to 325°F (165°C) and continue to cook 1 hour. Add carrots, parsnips, prunes, and apricots; continue cooking 30 minutes or until veal and vegetables are tender. Remove brisket to warm serving platter; surround with carrots, parsnips, and fruit. Keep warm. Pour cooking liquid into 1-cup glass measure. Skim and discard fat from cooking liquid. Add enough apple juice to equal 1 cup. Dissolve cornstarch in combined liquids; return to Dutch oven. Cook over medium-high heat until thickened, stirring constantly. Trim excess fat from brisket; carve brisket across the grain into thin slices. Serve with vegetables, fruit, and sauce. Serves 6.

Approximate nutritional analysis per serving:
Calories 344, Protein 30 g,
Carbohydrates 39 g, Fat 8 g,
Cholesterol 100 mg, Sodium 470 mg

Courtesy of the National Livestock and Meat Board.

Opposite:
Braised Veal Brisket with Dried Fruit

TOMATO, RICE, AND BEAN SOUP

1 cup (240 ml) onions, diced
1 cup (240 ml) carrots, diced
1 cup (240 ml) celery, diced
1 tbs (15 ml) butter or margarine
6 - 8 oz cans (1.4 l) GOYA Tomato Sauce
2 packets GOYA Beef Bouillon
1 tsp (5 ml) GOYA Adobo
1 packet Sazón GOYA sin Achiote
1 cup (240 ml) cooked white rice
1 - 16 oz can (480 g) GOYA Black Beans, rinsed and drained
pinch sugar
1 cup (240 ml) half-and-half or lowfat milk
salt and pepper to taste

In stockpot, sauté diced vegetables in butter on low heat until golden. Add tomato sauce, bouillon, Adobo, Sazón and bring to a boil. Cover pot and simmer 10 minutes. In blender, purée mixture in batches and return to pot. Add rice, beans, sugar and simmer 5 minutes more. Add half-and-half and simmer another 5 minutes. Do not boil. Serves 6–8.

Approximate nutritional analysis per serving:
Calories 342, Protein 14 g,
Carbohydrates 44 g, Fat 15 g,
Cholesterol 36 mg, Sodium 589 mg

OKTOBERFEST RIBS

- 2 - 32 oz jars (1.9 kg) sauerkraut, drained
- 2 yellow onions, peeled and cut in half
- 2 tart green apples, cored and wedged
- ¼ cup (60 ml) brown sugar
- 2 lbs (910 g) pork ribs
- 8 juniper berries *or* 1 tbs (15 ml) caraway seed

Layer ingredients into a large Dutch oven in this order: sauerkraut, onions, apples, brown sugar (sprinkle evenly over), and ribs. Bury juniper berries or caraway seed evenly in the sauerkraut layer. Bring to boil, lower heat, cover and simmer gently for 2–3 hours, until ribs are very tender. Serves 6.

Approximate nutritional analysis per serving: Calories 315, Protein 19 g, Carbohydrates 29 g, Fat 14 g, Cholesterol 54 mg, Sodium 1130 mg

Courtesy of the National Pork Producers Council.

CALDO GALLEGA
White Bean Soup

- 4 packets GOYA Chicken Bouillon
- 8 cups (1.9 l) water
- 2 GOYA Chorizos, sliced
- 3 potatoes, peeled and cubed
- 3 turnips, peeled and sliced
- ½ lb (230 g) smoked ham, diced
- ½ lb (230 g) fresh kale, broccoli rabe, or turnip greens, chopped
- 1 onion, sliced
- 1 - 16 oz can (480 g) GOYA Small White Beans
- ½ tsp (3 ml) GOYA Adobo with Pepper
- 1 packet Sazón GOYA sin Achiote

In a large saucepan, combine chicken bouillon, water, chorizo, potatoes, turnips, ham, kale, and onion. Bring to a boil, reduce heat, and simmer, covered, for 50 minutes. Add beans, Adobo, and Sazón. Simmer, covered, for 10 more minutes, or until potatoes are tender. Serves 6.

Approximate nutritional analysis per serving: Calories 411, Protein 18 g, Carbohydrates 28 g, Fat 33 g, Cholesterol 55 mg, Sodium 786 mg

Opposite: Caldo Gallega

Octoberfest Ribs

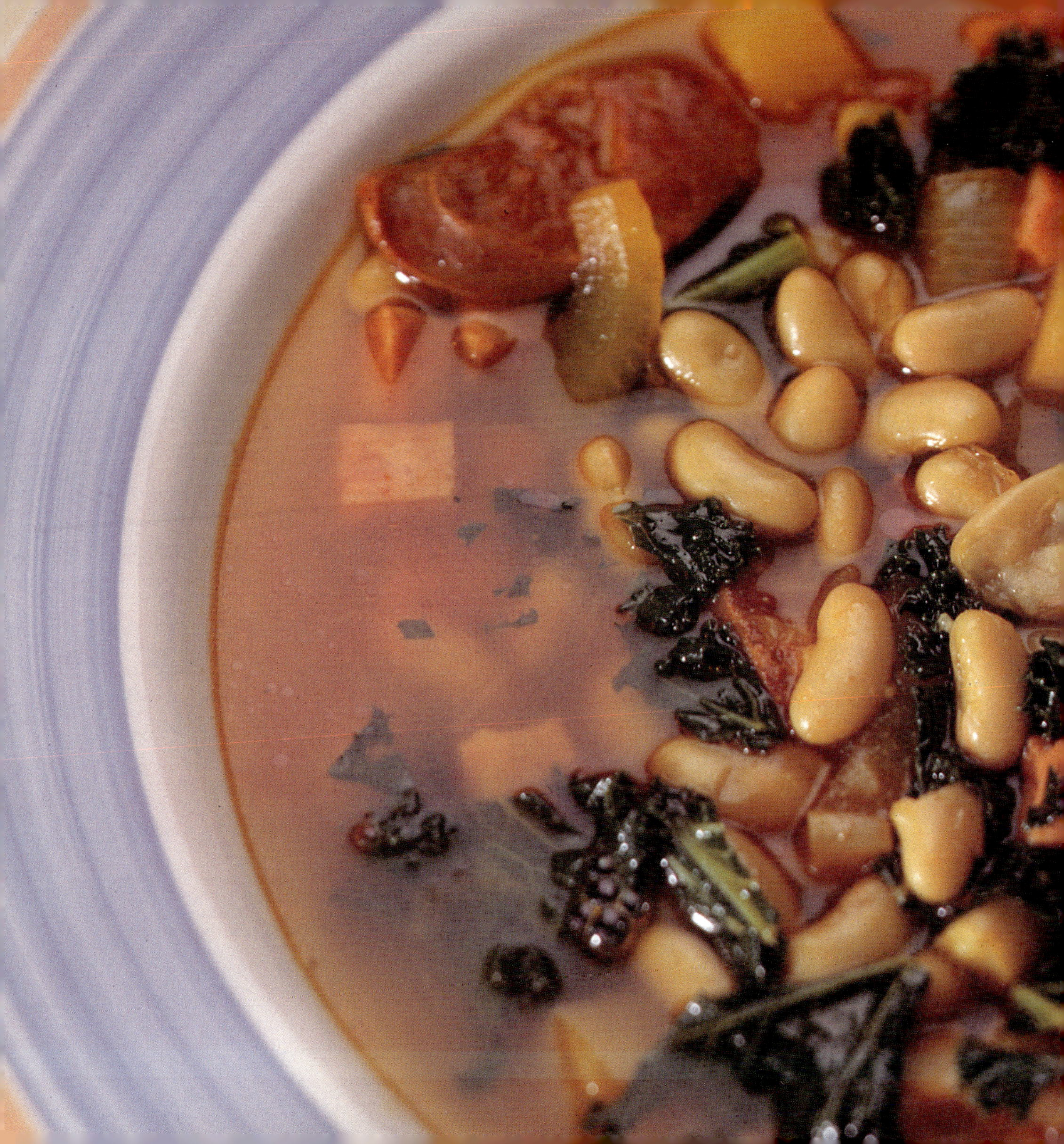

FIESTA PORK CHOPS

4 pork chops, ¾-inch thick
1 tbs (15 ml) vegetable oil
1 - 6.8 oz pkg. (204 g)
    RICE-A-RONI Spanish Rice
2 tbs (30 ml) margarine or butter
2 cups (480 ml) hot water
1 - 8 oz can (240 ml) tomato sauce
2 tomatoes, seeded, chopped
1 medium onion, chopped
1–2 jalapeño peppers, chopped

In large skillet, brown pork chops in oil. Drain; set aside. In same skillet, combine Rice-A-Roni mix and margarine. Sauté until golden brown. Stir in water, contents of seasoning packet, tomato sauce, tomatoes, onion, and pepper. Layer pork chops over rice mixture in skillet; bring to a boil. Cover; reduce heat. Simmer 30 minutes or until liquid is absorbed and rice and chops are tender. Serves 4.

Approximate nutritional analysis per serving: Calories 475, Protein 35 g, Carbohydrates 47 g, Fat 16 g, Cholesterol 80 mg, Sodium 975 mg

CHICKEN CORN CHOWDER

1 - 3 lb (1.4 kg) EMPIRE
    KOSHER Chicken with neck
    and giblets
1 medium onion, chopped
1 stalk celery, chopped
2 large carrots, chopped
1 - 16 oz can (480 g) corn kernels
    with liquid
1 - 32 oz can (960 g) whole
    tomatoes, drained and cut up
1 tsp (5 ml) lemon juice
salt and pepper

Bring chicken to a boil in 4 cups water. Skim. Simmer with onion, celery, and carrots until tender, about 45 minutes. Remove chicken, let cool. Discard skin and bones, cut meat in bite-size pieces, along with giblets if desired. Skim fat from chicken broth. Combine chicken meat, broth, corn, tomatoes, and lemon juice. Season with salt and pepper, simmer for 30–45 minutes. Serves 4.

Approximate nutritional analysis per serving: Calories 781, Protein 103 g, Carbohydrates 32 g, Fat 26 g, Cholesterol 301 mg, Sodium 787 mg

Chicken Corn Chowder

BUTIFARRA CON ALUBIAS
White Beans with Sausage

1 lb (455 g) sweet sausages
1 tbs (15 ml) GOYA Olive Oil
1 small onion, chopped
4 cloves garlic, minced
3 strips bacon, chopped
2 - 16 oz cans (960 g) GOYA Small White Beans
2 tbs (30 ml) GOYA Sofrito
1 bay leaf
½ tsp (3 ml) GOYA Adobo with Pepper
2 tbs (30 ml) chopped parsley
1 whole GOYA Pimiento, cut into strips

Puncture sausages with fork, and sauté in a large skillet in olive oil until well browned. Remove sausages and set aside. In the same pan, sauté onion, garlic, and bacon until bacon is browned. Add beans, Sofrito, and bay leaf, and simmer 2–3 minutes over low–medium heat, stirring often. Stir in Adobo and parsley. Arrange sausages and pimiento strips on top. Remove bay leaf.
Serves 6.

Approximate nutritional analysis per serving: Calories 478, Protein 25 g, Carbohydrates 31 g, Fat 28 g, Cholesterol 66 mg, Sodium 789 mg

HEARTY BEEF VEGETABLE STEW

- 2 tsp (10 ml) OLD BAY Seasoning or more to taste, divided
- 3 lbs (1.4 kg) beef chuck roast, trimmed of fat, cut into chunks
- 4 large potatoes, peeled and cut into chunks
- 3 carrots, scraped and sliced
- 1 cup (240 ml) water

Sprinkle 1 tsp Old Bay Seasoning over beef. Sprinkle remaining tsp Old Bay Seasoning over vegetables. To crockpot, add water, chuck roast chunks, and vegetables; cook on high for 6 hours. Serves 10.

Approximate nutritional analysis per serving: Calories 417, Protein 44 g, Carbohydrates 14 g, Fat 20 g, Cholesterol 144 mg, Sodium 161 mg

YAMBILEE BEEF STEW

- ⅓ cup (80 ml) all-purpose flour
- 1½ tsp (8 ml) salt, divided
- 2 lbs (190 g) stew beef, cut into 1-inch cubes
- ¼ cup (60 ml) salad oil
- 1 - 10½ oz can (315 ml) condensed beef broth (bouillon), undiluted
- 1 - 8 oz can (240 ml) tomato sauce
- ⅓ cup (80 ml) chopped fresh parsley
- 1 clove garlic, minced
- ½ tsp (3 ml) thyme leaves
- ½ tsp (3 ml) pepper
- ½ bay leaf
- 1 large onion, chopped
- 12 small whole white onions
- 3 cloves
- ½ cup (120 ml) dry sherry
- 4 medium uncooked LOUISIANA Yams*, pared and cut into 2-inch pieces
- 1 lb (455 g) fresh green beans**, cut in half
- 1 cup (240 ml) celery pieces

* 2 - 16 oz cans (960 ml) Louisiana Yams, drained and quartered, may be substituted for fresh yams. Add during last 20 minutes of cooking time.
** 2 - 9 oz pkgs. (540 g) frozen cut green beans may be substituted for fresh beans. Add during last 20 minutes of cooking time.

Opposite:
Hearty Beef Vegetable Stew

Combine ⅓ cup flour and ½ tsp salt in a small bag; add meat, a few pieces at a time, shake until evenly coated. In large Dutch oven, heat salad oil. Add meat and cook, a few pieces at a time, until well browned, removing pieces as they brown. Drain fat from Dutch oven.

Return meat to Dutch oven; add condensed beef broth, tomato sauce, parsley, garlic, thyme, 1 tsp salt, pepper, bay leaf, and chopped onion. In one small onion place 3 cloves and add to Dutch oven; set aside remaining 11 small whole white onions. Heat to boiling. Reduce heat to low; cover and simmer 1¼ hours, stirring occasionally. Add sherry, remaining 11 small whole white onions, yams, green beans, and celery; continue cooking for 45 minutes more or until vegetables are fork-tender.

If desired, thicken stew by removing ½ cup liquid from stew to a small bowl; blend in 1 tbs flour with the ½ cup liquid until smooth. Slowly stir flour mixture into stew. Stir frequently and simmer 5 minutes more or until stew is slightly thickened. Remove and discard cloves from onion. Serve stew in bowls. Serves 8.

Approximate nutritional analysis per serving: Calories 517, Protein 39 g, Carbohydrates 33 g, Fat 24 g, Cholesterol 120 mg, Sodium 248 mg

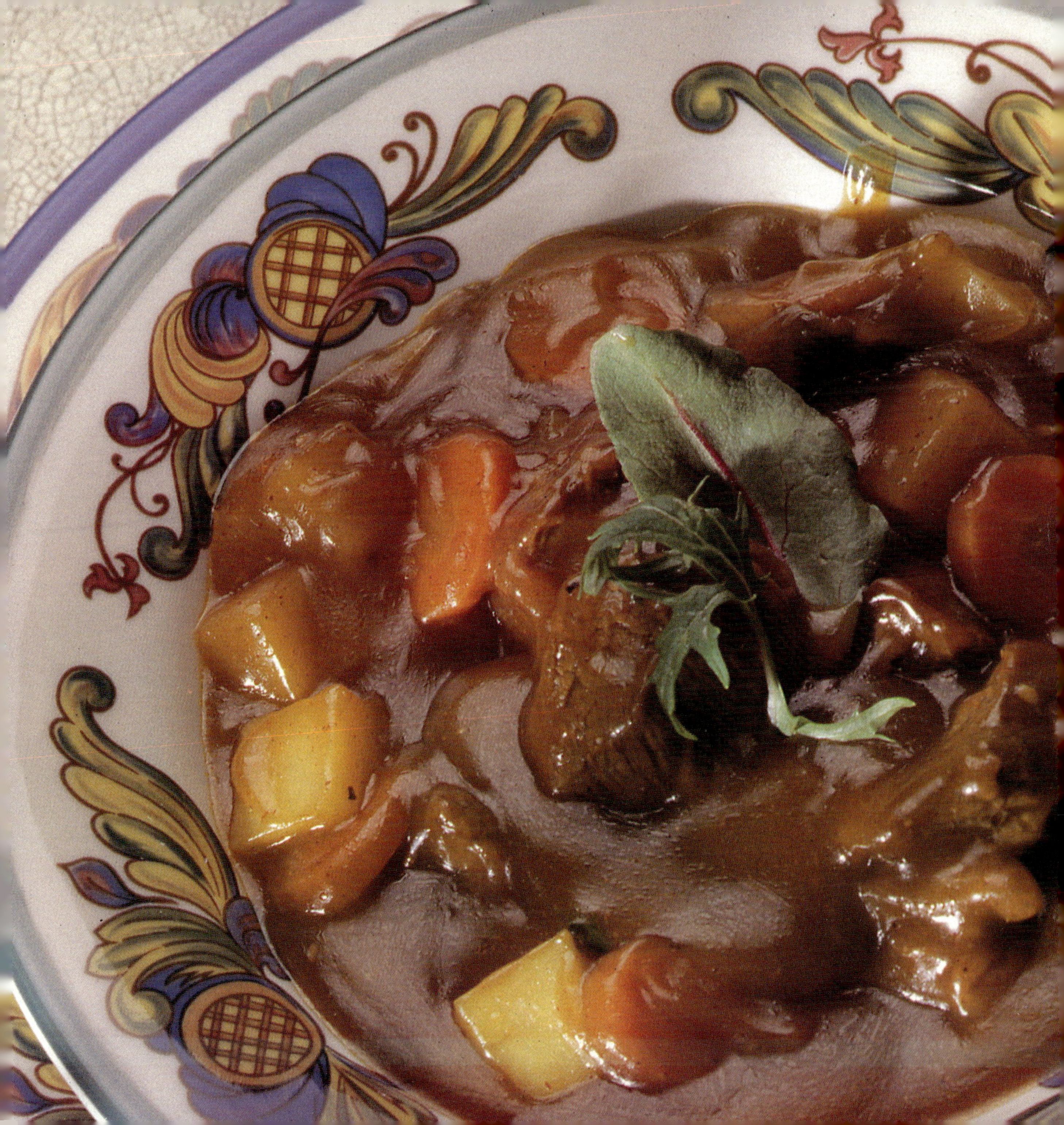

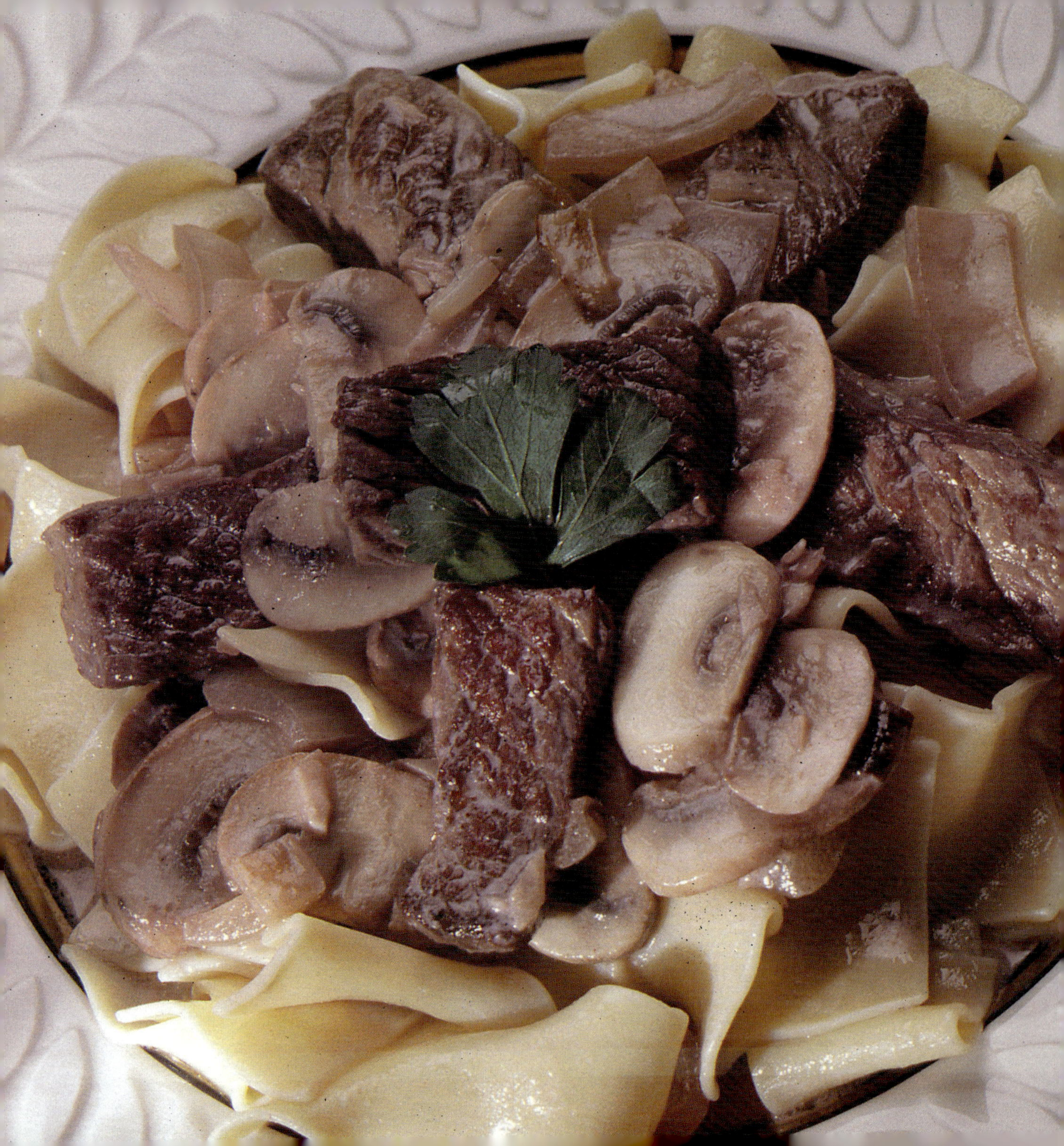

GYPSY GOULASH

1 lb (455 g) lean ground beef
4 tsp (20 ml) vegetable oil
3 green bell peppers, halved and sliced
2 medium onions, sliced
2 tbs (30 ml) paprika
1 lb (455 g) tomatoes, halved and sliced
½ cup (120 ml) sliced CALIFORNIA Ripe Olives
salt and pepper
boiled potatoes, optional

Sauté beef in large skillet in 2 tsp oil over high heat until browned. Remove meat from pan, leaving drippings. Add 2 tsp oil, the peppers, and onion to pan and sauté over high heat about 5 minutes or until tender. Stir in paprika. Return beef to pan, add tomatoes and olives and heat through. Salt and pepper to taste. Serve in wide soup bowls with thickly sliced boiled potatoes, if desired. Serves 4.

Approximate nutritional analysis per serving: Calories 448, Protein 31 g, Carbohydrates 21 g, Fat 27 g, Cholesterol 99 mg, Sodium 195 mg

Opposite: Beef Stroganoff

BEEF STROGANOFF

1 tbs (15 ml) butter or margarine
½ cup (120 ml) chopped onion
1 clove garlic, finely chopped
1 lb (455 g) lean beef sirloin, ½ inch thick, cut into 3x½-inch strips
8 oz (240 g) mushrooms, sliced
¼ cup (60 ml) dry red wine
2 tbs (30 ml) cornstarch
1 cup (240 ml) condensed beef broth
¼ tsp (1 ml) pepper
1 cup (240 ml) YOPLAIT Fat Free Plain Yogurt
hot cooked noodles or rice

Heat butter or margarine in 10-inch skillet until melted. Add onion and garlic; cook and stir over medium-high heat until tender. Add beef and mushrooms; cook and stir about 7 minutes or until beef is no longer pink. Stir in wine; reduce heat. Cover and simmer 10 minutes. Stir cornstarch into beef broth until smooth; stir into beef mixture. Cook and stir over medium-high heat until thickened; remove from heat. Stir in pepper and yogurt; heat through over low heat if necessary— do not boil. Serve over noodles or rice. Serves 4.

High altitude (3500–6500 ft): Thinly slice beef.

Approximate nutritional analysis per serving: Calories 500, Protein 42 g, Carbohydrates 57 g, Fat 11 g, Cholesterol 130 mg, Sodium 580 mg

Gypsy Goulash

STEWS • 15

COCIDO MADRILEÑO
Chick Pea Stew

1 - 16 oz can (480 g) GOYA Chick Peas, drained and rinsed
1 gal. (3.8 kg) water
4 new potatoes, peeled
1 lb (455 g) beef chunks
2 chicken thighs
¼ lb (115 g) bacon
1 GOYA Chorizo sausage
2 soup bones
1 ham hock, cut in pieces
1 small pork sparerib
1 sweet sausage
3 whole medium onions, peeled
1 large carrot, cut into 3 pieces
2 cloves garlic
1 leek, split
1 bay leaf
1 sprig fresh thyme
1 packet Sazón GOYA sin Achiote
2 tsp (10 ml) GOYA Adobo with Pepper
1 - 12 oz pkg. (360 g) GOYA Fideos, broken up

In a large soup pot, combine chick peas, water, potatoes, beef, chicken, bacon, chorizo, soup bones, ham hock, sparerib, sausage, onions, carrot, garlic, leek, bay leaf, thyme, Sazón, and Adobo. Bring to a boil, reduce heat, and simmer, covered, an additional 20 minutes. With a slotted spoon, carefully remove the chick peas, vegetables, and pieces of meat from soup and arrange on platter. Discard bay leaf and bones. Return stew to a boil, and cook pasta in stew until done. Serve stew next to platter of meat. Serves 8.

Approximate nutritional analysis per serving: Calories 728, Protein 50 g, Carbohydrates 39 g, Fat 40 g, Cholesterol 169 mg, Sodium 479 mg

PORK STEW WITH CORNBREAD DUMPLINGS

STEW:
1½ lbs (685 g) boneless pork, cut in 1-inch cubes
1 large onion, cut in wedges
1 clove garlic, minced
2 large carrots, cut in 1-inch slices
2 large potatoes, peeled and cut into large chunks
1 - 16 oz can (480 g) tomatoes, coarsely chopped
¼ cup (60 ml) strong coffee or beef broth
2 tbs (30 ml) molasses
1 tsp (5 ml) LEA & PERRINS Worcestershire sauce
2 tsp (10 ml) salt
½ tsp (3 ml) oregano, crushed
½ tsp (3 ml) thyme, crushed
dash cayenne pepper
¾ cup (180 ml) natural raisins

DUMPLINGS:
1 - 15 oz pkg. (450 g) cornbread mix
1 - 8 oz can (240 g) corn, drained

In 3-qt casserole combine all stew ingredients except raisins. Cover and microwave on HIGH until boiling, about 10 minutes. Reduce power to MEDIUM and continue cooking, covered, for 1 hour. Stir in raisins.

Dumplings: Mix cornbread as directed, reducing liquid called for by ¼ cup. Stir in drained corn. Drop tablespoonfuls of corn batter over surface of hot stew, leaving center open. Microwave, uncovered, on MEDIUM-HIGH for 5–6 minutes, rotating dish a half turn after 3 minutes. Dumplings expand and blend into each other. Test dumplings for doneness using a pick. Serves 6.

Approximate nutritional analysis per serving (stew only): Calories 435, Protein 40 g, Carbohydrates 37 g, Fat 14 g, Cholesterol 129 mg, Sodium 972 mg

Approximate nutritional analysis per serving (dumplings only): Calories 192, Protein 5 g, Carbohydrates 41 g, Fat 1 g, Cholesterol 0 mg, Sodium 909 mg

Opposite:
Pork Stew with Cornbread Dumplings

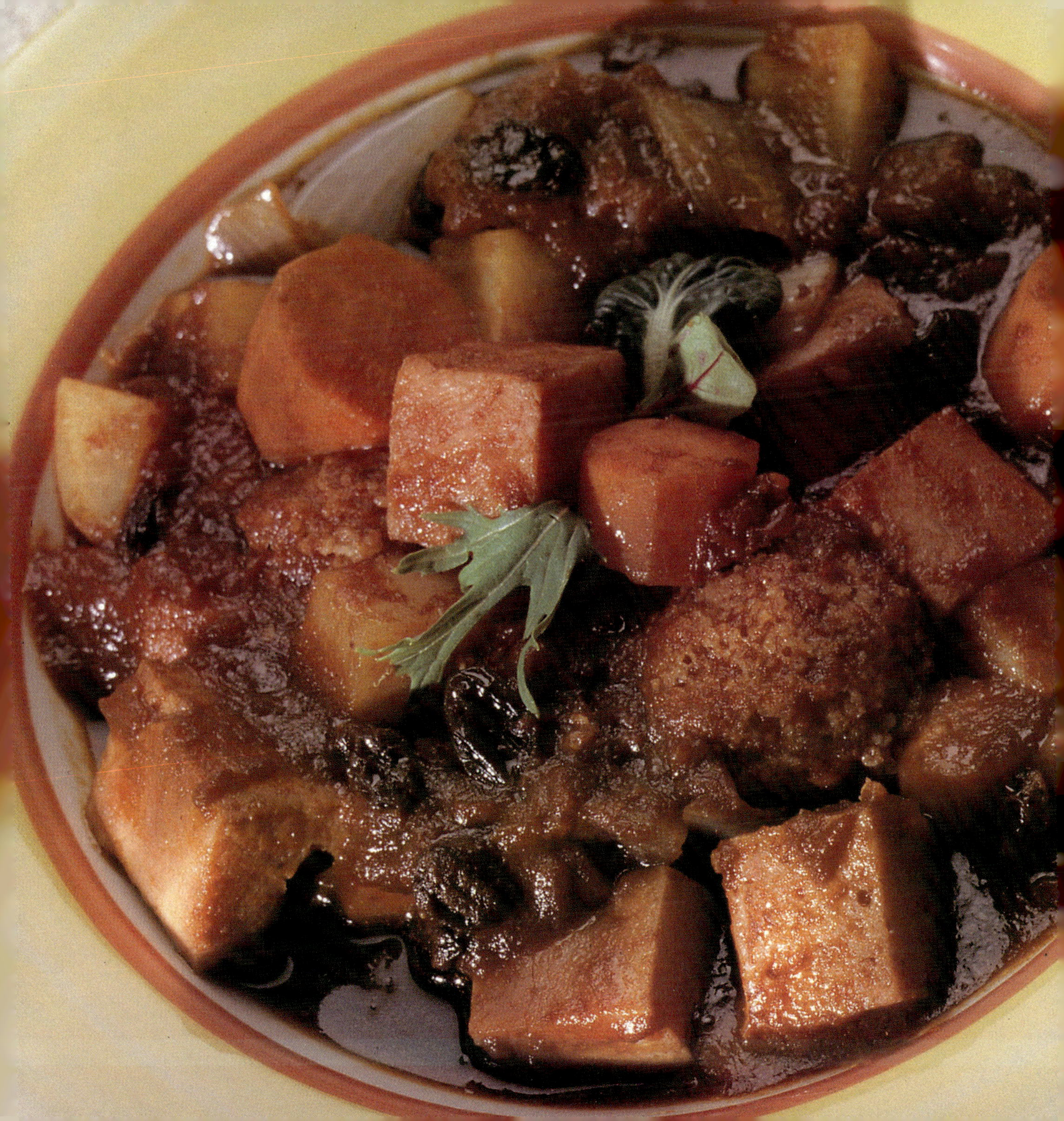

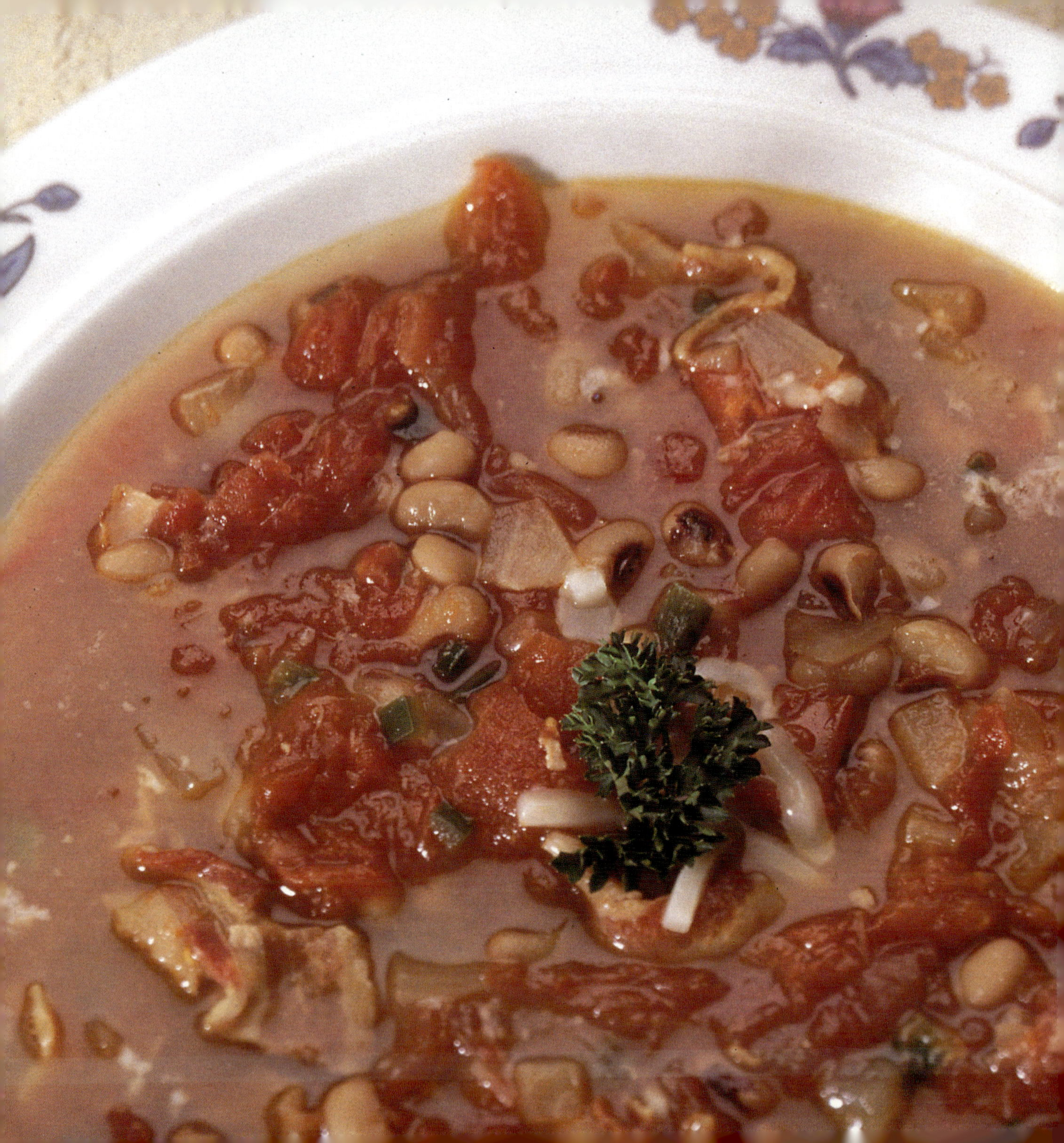

VEAL AND VEGETABLE SOUP

1½ lbs (685 g) veal for stew, cut into 1-inch pieces
2 cloves garlic, minced
1 tbs (15 ml) olive oil, divided
½ tsp (3 ml) salt
3½ cups (840 ml) water
1 - 13¾ oz can (410 ml) ready-to-serve beef broth
1 tbs (15 ml) fresh marjoram leaves, crushed
   or 1½ tsp (8 ml) dried marjoram leaves, crushed
¼ tsp (1 ml) coarse grind black pepper
½ lb (230 g) red potatoes, cut into ½-inch cubes
1½ cups (355 ml) fresh corn kernels or frozen whole kernel corn
1 small zucchini

Combine veal for stew and minced garlic; reserve. Heat 2 tsp oil in Dutch oven or large deep saucepan over medium heat. Brown veal, ½ lb at a time, using remaining oil as needed. Pour off drippings, if necessary. Sprinkle veal with salt. Return veal to pan; add water, beef broth, marjoram, and pepper. Bring to a boil; reduce heat to low. Cover and simmer 45 minutes. Add potatoes and corn; continue simmering, covered, 15 minutes or until veal and vegetables are tender. Meanwhile cut zucchini in half lengthwise; cut crosswise into ¼-inch slices. Add zucchini to pan; continue cooking, covered, 5 minutes or until zucchini is crisp-tender. Serves 6.

Approximate nutritional analysis per serving: Calories 234, Protein 25 g, Carbohydrates 16 g, Fat 8 g, Cholesterol 93 mg, Sodium 477 mg

Courtesy of the National Livestock and Meat Board.

Opposite: Black-Eyed Pea Soup

BLACK-EYED PEA SOUP

5–6 slices bacon, cut in small pieces and fried
1 cup (240 ml) onion, chopped
2 tbs (30 ml) jalapeños, seeds removed, finely chopped
2 cups (480 ml) Italian-style tomatoes, chopped
1 garlic clove, minced and mashed
1 tsp (5 ml) IMPERIAL Granulated Sugar
pinch salt and pepper
2 - 15½ oz cans (930 ml) beef broth
4 - 15½ oz cans (1.9 kg) black-eyed peas, drained
3 cups (720 ml) cheddar or Swiss cheese, grated
additional cheese for garnish

Fry bacon in soup kettle until lightly browned; add onion, jalapeños, tomatoes, garlic, sugar, salt, and pepper. Sauté in bacon drippings over medium-high heat, about 5 minutes. Add beef broth and black-eyed peas; stir and simmer about 15 minutes. At serving time, add cheese and simmer gently until cheese is melted. Sprinkle each serving with additional cheese. Serves 10.

Approximate nutritional analysis per serving: Calories 355, Protein 15 g, Carbohydrates 31 g, Fat 19 g, Cholesterol 44 mg, Sodium 648 mg

STEWS • 19

A QUICKIE CASSOULET

3 tbs (45 ml) GOYA Corn Oil or butter
2 cups (480 ml) tomatoes, chopped
6 shallots, sliced
2 cloves garlic, minced
2 tbs (30 ml) parsley, chopped
2 - 15 oz cans (850 g) GOYA White Kidney Beans, drained
1 lb (455 g) Italian sausage, cooked

Heat corn oil or melt butter in skillet; add tomatoes, shallots, garlic, and parsley. Sauté until tender. Combine with beans in a 2-qt casserole, top with sausage and bake at 350°F (180°C) for 30 minutes. Serves 4.

Approximate nutritional analysis per serving: Calories 758, Protein 37 g, Carbohydrates 48 g, Fat 47 g, Cholesterol 94 mg, Sodium 348 mg

CALERETA DE PASTOR
Shepherd's Lamb Stew

2 cloves garlic, peeled
3 tbs (45 ml) GOYA Olive Oil
1½ lbs (685 g) boneless lamb, cut into 1-inch cubes
1 tsp (5 ml) GOYA Adobo with Cumin
1 onion, chopped
1 bay leaf
1 tomato, cut in chunks
2 carrots, peeled and sliced
1 cup (240 ml) LA VINA Red Cooking Wine
1 packet GOYA Chicken Bouillon
1 cup (240 ml) water
1 clove
1 peppercorn
1 tsp (5 ml) chopped GOYA Green Jalapeños
1½ tsp (8 ml) ground almonds
1 slice toasted bread
1 tbs (15 ml) GOYA Red Wine Vinegar
2 tsp (10 ml) paprika
1 whole GOYA Pimiento
1 packet Sazón GOYA sin Achiote
½ tsp (3 ml) fresh thyme, minced

In a large flame-proof casserole or Dutch oven, sauté garlic in olive oil until brown. Remove garlic with a slotted spoon and set aside. Sprinkle lamb cubes evenly with Adobo. In same casserole or Dutch oven, sauté lamb cubes, onion, and bay leaf until lamb is browned. Add tomato, carrots, red cooking wine, bouillon, and water. Bring to a boil, reduce heat, and simmer, uncovered, for 30 minutes.

In separate bowl, mash together clove, peppercorn, jalapeños, almonds, toasted bread, vinegar, paprika, pimiento, browned garlic, and Sazón. Remove ⅓ cup of stew liquid from casserole, add to spice mixture in bowl, and stir. Add this mixture back into casserole and stir. Bring to a boil, and boil, uncovered, for 3–4 minutes. Remove bay leaf. Garnish with fresh thyme and serve. Serves 6.

Approximate nutritional analysis per serving: Calories 350, Protein 34 g, Carbohydrates 10 g, Fat 3 g, Cholesterol 101 mg, Sodium 370 mg

Opposite: A Quickie Cassoulet

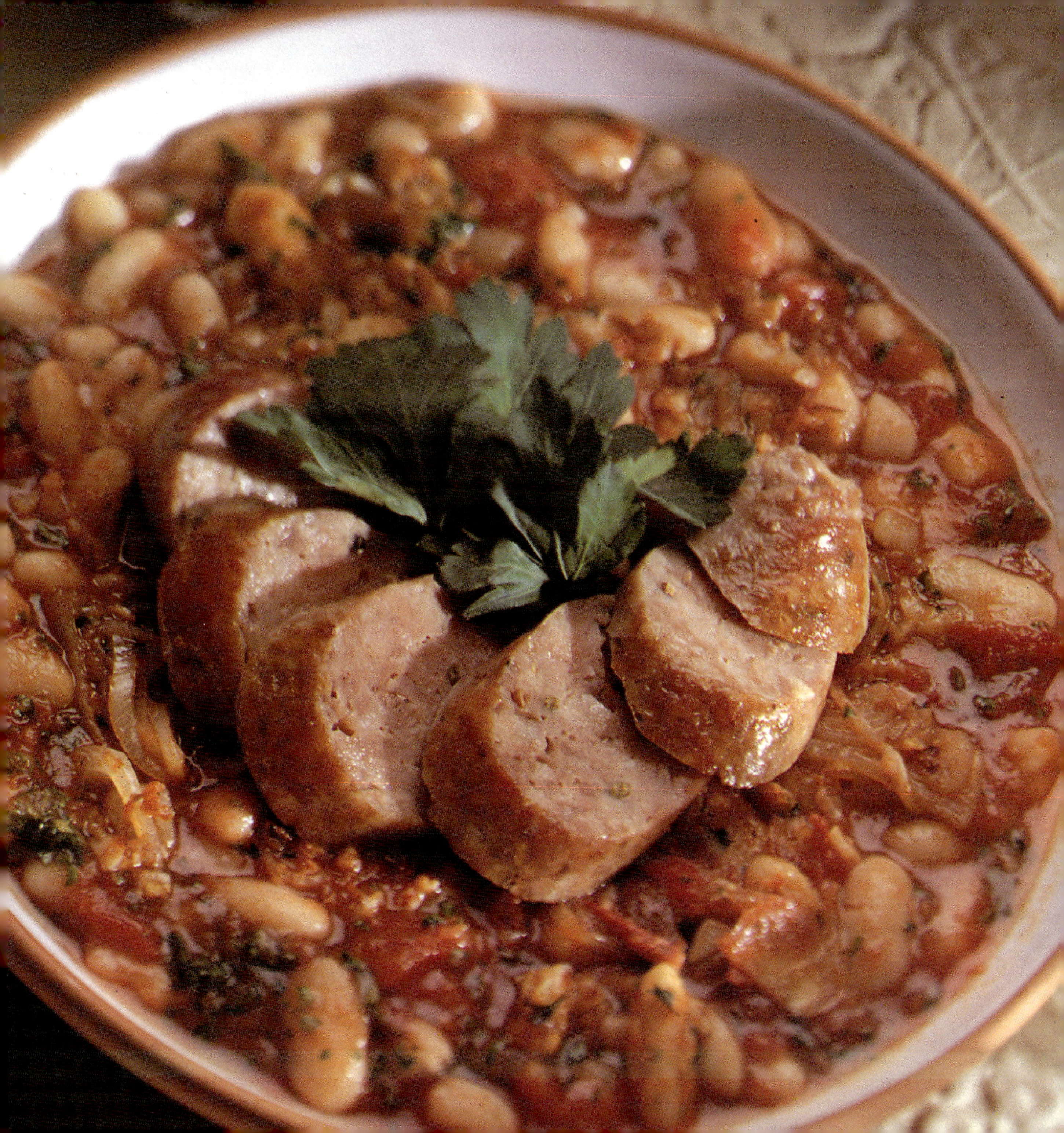

MOUNTAIN CHILI

2 lbs (910 g) beef sirloin, cut into 1-inch pieces
12 oz (360 g) pork sausage links, cut into 1-inch pieces
2 tbs (30 ml) vegetable oil
2 - 16 oz jars (960 g) CHI-CHI'S Salsa
1 - 10½ oz can (315 ml) beef consommé
1 cup (240 ml) beer
1 cup (240 ml) chopped green bell pepper
1 cup (240 ml) chopped red bell pepper
1 cup (240 ml) chopped onion
1 - 6 oz can (180 g) tomato paste
2 bay leaves
1 tbs plus 1½ tsp (23 ml) chili powder
4 tsp (20 ml) ground cumin
4 tsp (20 ml) minced fresh garlic
1 tsp (5 ml) dried oregano leaves
1 tsp (5 ml) sugar
¾ tsp (4 ml) pepper
sour cream
shredded cheddar cheese
chopped avocado

In Dutch oven, brown beef and sausage in oil. Drain. Stir in remaining ingredients except sour cream, cheese, and avocado. Bring to a boil; reduce heat to low. Simmer, stirring occasionally, 1½ hours or until beef is tender. Serve with sour cream, shredded cheese, and chopped avocado. Serves 9.

Approximate nutritional analysis per serving: Calories 280, Protein 24 g, Carbohydrates 16 g, Fat 13 g, Cholesterol 65 mg, Sodium 108 mg

BLACK BEAN CHILI

1½ lbs (685 g) ground beef
1 cup (240 ml) chopped onions
1 clove garlic, minced
2 - 16 oz cans (960 ml) black beans, drained
1 - 1¼ oz packet (38 g) ORTEGA Taco Seasoning Mix
1 - 12 oz jar (360 g) ORTEGA Mild, Medium, or Hot Thick and Chunky Salsa
1 cup (240 ml) water
1 cup (240 ml) shredded cheese

In large saucepan, over medium-high heat, cook beef, onions, and garlic until beef is no longer pink, stirring occasionally to break up meat; drain. Add black beans, taco seasoning mix, salsa, and water. Cover; heat to boil. Reduce heat; simmer 20 minutes. Serve chili topped with cheese. Serves 8.

Approximate nutritional analysis per serving: Calories 331, Protein 27 g, Carbohydrates 14 g, Fat 18 g, Cholesterol 66 mg, Sodium 898 mg

Mountain Chili

SEAFOOD STEW

- 1 cup (240 ml) shredded carrots
- 1 cup (240 ml) sliced celery
- 1 cup (240 ml) sliced leeks
- 2 tsp (10 ml) minced fresh garlic
- ¼ cup (60 ml) butter or margarine
- 2 cups (480 ml) water
- 1 cup (240 ml) clam juice
- 1 - 8 oz jar (240 ml) CHI-CHI'S Salsa
- 1 cup (240 ml) dry white wine
- 2 cups (480 ml) cubed baking potatoes, 1 inch
- 2 bay leaves
- ½ tsp (3 ml) seafood seasoning mix
- ½ tsp (93 ml) dried thyme leaves
- ¼ tsp (1 ml) coarsely ground pepper
- 1 lb (455 g) fresh or frozen raw shrimp, deveined and rinsed
- 1 lb (455 g) white fish fillets (halibut, scrod, etc.), cut into 1-inch pieces
- 1 - 6 oz pkg. (180 g) frozen cooked crab meat, thawed
- ½ lb (230 g) bacon, cooked and crumbled

In Dutch oven, cook carrots, celery, leeks, and garlic in butter 8–10 minutes or until vegetables are softened. Add water, clam juice, salsa, wine, potatoes, bay leaves, seasoning mix, thyme, and pepper. Bring to a boil. Reduce heat to medium-low. Cover; cook 30–40 minutes or until potatoes are just tender, stirring occasionally. Add shrimp, fish, and crab meat. Cook 4–5 minutes or just until shrimp turn pink, stirring occasionally. Stir in bacon. Remove bay leaves. Serves 9.

Seafood Stew

Approximate nutritional analysis per serving: Calories 270, Protein 26 g, Carbohydrates 12 g, Fat 11 g, Cholesterol 105 mg, Sodium 650 mg

BAYOU JAMBALAYA

1 medium onion, sliced
½ cup (120 ml) chopped green pepper
1 clove garlic, minced
2 tbs (30 ml) vegetable oil
1 cup (240 ml) uncooked white rice
¾ cup (180 ml) HEINZ Tomato Ketchup
2 cups (480 ml) water
1 tbs (15 ml) HEINZ Vinegar
⅛ tsp (.5 ml) black pepper
⅛ tsp (.5 ml) red pepper
1 medium tomato, coarsely chopped
1 cup (240 ml) cooked ham
½ lb (230 g) raw shrimp, shelled and deveined

Microwave Directions: Place onion, green pepper, garlic, and oil in 3-qt casserole. Cover dish with lid or vented plastic wrap; microwave on HIGH 3–4 minutes, stirring once. Stir in rice, ketchup, water, vinegar, black pepper, red pepper, tomato, and ham. Cover; microwave on HIGH 10–12 minutes or until mixture comes to a boil. Microwave on MEDIUM 18–20 minutes until rice is cooked, stirring once. Stir in shrimp; cover. Microwave on HIGH 2–3 minutes or until shrimp turn pink. Let stand, covered, 5 minutes before serving.

Stovetop: In large skillet, sauté first 4 ingredients in oil until onion is transparent. Stir in ketchup and remaining ingredients except shrimp. Cover; simmer 20–25 minutes or until rice is tender. Add shrimp; simmer uncovered 3–5 minutes or until shrimp turn pink, stirring occasionally. Serves 6.

Bayou Jambalaya

Approximate nutritional analysis per serving: Calories 243, Protein 29 g, Carbohydrates 18 g, Fat 6 g, Cholesterol 66 mg, Sodium 148 mg

STEWS

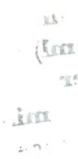

Copyright © 1997 Tripart, Ltd.
All Rights Reserved. No part of this book may be reproduced or copied in any format without written permission from the publisher. Popular Brands Cookbooks™ is a trademark of
MODERN PUBLISHING
A Division of Unisystems, Inc. / New York, New York 10022
Printed in the U.S.A.

Note: Although the recipes contained in this book have been tested by the manufacturers and have been carefully edited by the publisher, the publisher and the manufacturers cannot be held responsible for any ill effects caused by errors in the recipes, or by spoiled ingredients, unsanitary conditions, incorrect preparation procedures or any other cause beyond their control.